DISCARD

21st Century Skills Library

COOL SCIENCE CAREERS

Storm Chaser

Ann Heinrichs

Cherry Lake Publishing
Ann Arbor, Michigan

Published in the United States of America by Cherry Lake Publishing
Ann Arbor, Michigan
www.cherrylakepublishing.com

Content Adviser: Warren Faidley, CEO and President, Weatherstock Inc.

Photo Credits: Cover and pages 1 and 4, ©AP Photo/Hays Daily News, Steven Hausler;
page 6, ©iStockphoto.com/clintspencer; page 11, ©iStockphoto.com/lisafx; page 12,
©iStockphoto.com/diane39; page 16, ©Ilene MacDonald/Alamy; page 19, ©AP Photo/Dave
Martin; page 20, ©Stock Connection Blue/Alamy; page 23, ©A.T. Willett/Alamy; page 24,
©AP Photo/The News-Gazette, Francis Gardler; page 26, ©Reven T.C. Wurman/Alamy

Library of Congress Cataloging-in-Publication Data
Heinrichs, Ann.
Storm chaser / by Ann Heinrichs.
    p. cm.—(Cool science careers)
Includes index.
ISBN-13: 978-1-60279-308-8
ISBN-10: 1-60279-308-5
1. Tornadoes—Juvenile literature. 2. Extreme sports—Juvenile
literature. I. Title.
QC941.3.H45 2008
551.55—dc22   2008029289

Cherry Lake Publishing would like to acknowledge the work of
The Partnership for 21st Century Skills.
Please visit www.21stcenturyskills.org for more information.

TABLE OF CONTENTS

CHAPTER ONE

TWISTER!

Storm chasers get close to storms so they can take pictures and collect data.

"Twister!" yells the **radar** operator. The storm chasers pile into the van and off they go, tearing across the plains. The air seems electric as an eerie darkness fills the sky. Suddenly they spot it—a twisty black cloud snaking from the sky to the ground. How close can they get without being sucked into the whirling storm?

Storm chasing is exciting. Most storm chasers are ordinary people fascinated by weather. They may travel hundreds of miles just to see a storm. They love the adventure, the thrill, and even the danger. For them, storm chasing is a **hobby** or an extreme sport. Some storm chasers are members of film crews. They want to capture exciting storm scenes for TV shows and videos.

Some storm chasers are also meteorologists. Meteorologists are scientists who study the weather. They try to predict storms so they can warn people to stay out of danger. The weather reporter at your local radio or TV station might be a meteorologist. Many meteorologists work for city, state, or national weather centers.

Storm chasers mostly chase tornadoes. A tornado is a violent storm with a column of air that whirls around in a circle. Observers see it as a dark, **funnel**-shaped cloud reaching down to the ground. This spinning funnel of

A twister can be an amazing sight, but it is also extremely dangerous. Be sure to head for safety when one is spotted nearby.

air is called a vortex. Tornadoes are also called twisters because of their coiling wind pattern. Wind speeds inside the vortex can reach as high as 300 miles (483 kilometers) per hour. Such high winds can throw a car into the air!

Tornadoes strike in countries all over the world. But the United States gets more tornadoes than anywhere else. About 1,000 tornadoes are reported there every year.

Most of them take place in a zone called Tornado Alley. It stretches from north to south across the central United States. Southeastern states get many tornadoes, too. The top five tornado states are Texas, Oklahoma, Florida, Kansas, and Nebraska. Tornadoes can happen at any time of the day or night. They can also occur at any time of the year. In Tornado Alley, the heaviest tornado season is April through June.

Have you seen the movie *The Wizard of Oz*? It begins in Kansas, smack dab in the middle of Tornado Alley. A twister picks up Dorothy and her dog, Toto, and sets them down in a faraway land. When Dorothy wakes up, she finds herself among the Munchkins and talking trees. Dorothy looks at Toto and says, "I've a feeling we're not in Kansas anymore."

Real tornadoes may not move things as far away as Oz. But they do lift objects up and set them down somewhere

else. A 1915 tornado in Kansas swept a sack of flour more than 100 miles (161 km) away!

People began chasing storms as a hobby in the 1950s. Roger Jensen of North Dakota got hooked on storms as a young man. He went on to chase and photograph all the storms he could find. Another North Dakotan, David Hoadley, is known as the father of storm chasing. He founded *Storm Track*, the first storm-chaser magazine. Neil Ward was the first to connect his storm-chasing hobby with meteorologists. While chasing a 1961 tornado in Oklahoma, he passed on information to the state weather bureau.

Meanwhile, the U.S. government was tracking storms, too. In 1959, the National Weather Bureau (now the National Weather Service) began using weather radars. The first weather **satellite** was launched in 1960. Using satellites and weather radars, the government could track weather conditions from space.

In 1964, the National Severe Storms Laboratory (NSSL) opened in Norman, Oklahoma. NSSL began its Tornado **Intercept** Project (TIP) in 1972. This was the nation's first large system for scientific storm chasing. NSSL went on to develop Doppler weather radars. They can detect wind and raindrop patterns that show where a tornado is forming.

21st Century Content

In the 1960s, people around the country began working as **volunteer** storm spotters. Spotters report severe weather conditions to their local weather bureaus or emergency management groups. Unlike storm chasers, storm spotters do not travel around. They stay in their local areas and keep close ties with weather and rescue agencies. The National Weather Service holds training classes for storm spotters. They play a valuable, life-saving role in their communities.

Warren Faidley was the first nonscientist to chase storms as a full-time job. He began his career in the 1980s as a newspaper reporter and photographer. Faidley started the first company that sold photos and videos of severe storms.

The disaster movie *Twister* came out in 1996. Meteorologists say that the movie is full of scientific errors. Still, it unleashed a flood of new **amateur** chasers. Storm chaser TV shows in the early 2000s inspired even more chasing. Now thousands of people spring into action when they hear that magic word—*twister*!

CHAPTER TWO

CHASING STORMS FOR A LIVING

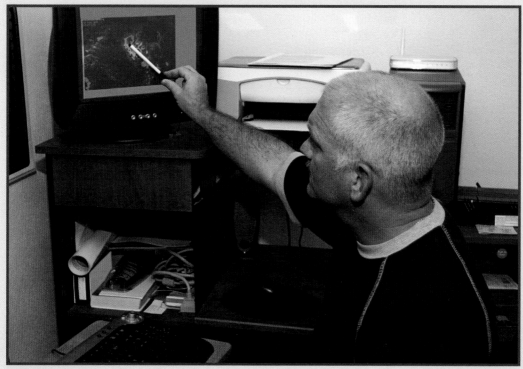

When they are not chasing storms, storm chasers conduct their own weather research.

Storm chasers chase tornadoes for only a few months a year. What do they do the rest of the time? If they are scientists, they work in **research labs**. Most storm-chasing scientists are meteorologists. In their labs, they study storms and how to detect them. These off-season

Doppler radar systems are used to help scientists spot storm formations. Here a Doppler radar tower scans the sky.

studies are valuable. No one would be able to chase storms without reliable weather information. Most of that information comes from weather centers and research labs run by the U.S. government.

The nation's top center for tornado research is the National Severe Storms Laboratory (NSSL). It works closely with the University of Oklahoma's Department of Meteorology. NSSL is part of the National Oceanic and Atmospheric Administration (NOAA). The Storm Prediction Center (SPC) works under the National Weather Service (NWS). Both the NSSL and the SPC are located in Norman, Oklahoma.

The Center for Severe Weather Research (CSWR) does tornado research, too. It's located in Boulder, Colorado. It often works on projects with the National Center for Atmospheric Research (NCAR), also in Boulder.

In the lab, a meteorologist's most important tool is the Doppler radar. It sends out signals that can detect both the location and speed of water droplets, which clouds are made of. Its screen shows images in colors that identify certain conditions. For example, red indicates heavy rain or hail. Lighter rain appears as yellow, green, and blue. In looking for a tornado, meteorologists first look for supercells. A supercell is a huge, spinning mass of clouds that creates a severe thunderstorm. It appears on the radar screen as a large, rotating, multicolored blob with a lot of red in the center. Supercells are the storms most likely to produce tornadoes.

The telltale sign of a tornado is a pattern called a Tornadic Vortex Signature (TVS). TVS is a curling, hook-shaped image that occurs when the Doppler radar finds a storm. Tornadoes typically move from the southwest toward the northeast. Once the meteorologist sees a TVS on the radar screen, he or she notifies the National Weather Service. The NWS then issues a tornado warning for that area.

Meteorology labs have a lot of other equipment and instruments. Many of these instruments display maps in

The Doppler radar system is monitored around the clock to help keep people safe from dangerous storms.

constant motion and charts with constant updates. They show weather conditions throughout the country and make **forecasts.** Some computer screens show images from weather satellites. Others have information from weather stations, weather balloons, or weather airplanes. Still, meteorologists say their best tools are their brains. They must understand what they're seeing and put it all together in a meaningful way.

Now let's move on to the chase! When tornado season arrives, some meteorologists go out looking for tornadoes. They may be studying how tornadoes begin, how they're structured, and how they behave. Or they may be testing new equipment.

Scientific storm-chasing groups are called intercept teams. At NSSL, the team members are NSSL meteorologists, University of Oklahoma students, and scientists from other labs or universities. All intercept teams take radar equipment with them into the field. The Doppler on Wheels (DOW), developed at the Boulder centers, is a useful device. So is NSSL's Shared Mobile Atmospheric Research and Teaching Radar (SMART-R). Both are Doppler radars mounted on trucks.

Intercept teams use sturdy vehicles to chase tornadoes. They're called tracking vehicles or chase vehicles. Some are vans, trucks, or sport utility vehicles (SUVs). Others may be specially built vehicles that almost look like military tanks. Chase vehicles are full of equipment. They may have a global positioning system (GPS) unit, scanners, monitors, two-way radios, satellite tracking instruments, camcorders, laptop computers, and an Internet connection. Intercept teams need all of these tools to collect and transmit data.

On the road, the team members may drive for hours and then sit waiting for hours. They watch their instruments to

One famous intercept team is made up of both meteorologists and filmmakers. The team leaders are meteorologist Josh Wurman and filmmaker Sean Casey. Casey designed and built his own tornado intercept vehicle (TIV). He took a pickup truck and stripped off the exterior. Then he added "armor"—8,000 pounds (3,629 kilograms) of steel plates. He hopes to drive the TIV right into the center of a tornado. This would produce awesome film shots. The TIV's instruments could also measure tornado conditions that have never been recorded before. This project has been featured on both the Discovery Channel and the National Geographic Channel.

see where a tornado might be forming. Then they speed to the location. Most of the time, the storm turns out to be just a severe thunderstorm.

When the team members do reach a tornado, they measure conditions such as wind speed, temperature, moisture, and **atmospheric pressure.** They may try to place equipment right in the tornado's path. When the project is over, they go back to work in their labs. With their new information, meteorologists become better at predicting tornadoes. That means they can help people to prepare and be safe when a tornado strikes.

CHAPTER THREE

BECOMING A STORM CHASER

Famous storm chaser Warren Faidley videotapes
Hurricane Isabel as it approaches the shore.

The urge to chase storms often starts in childhood. One **professional** storm chaser used to cut out weather maps from his local newspaper. One was hooked on tornadoes after he saw *The Wizard of Oz*. Another got interested in storms at age 12 when a flooded river swept him away!

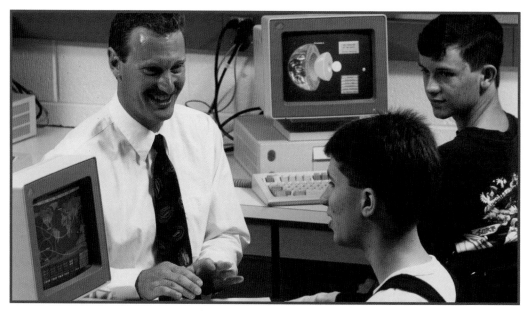

Students who study meteorology must learn how to interpret the satellite data and other information.

Maybe you'd enjoy storm chasing as a hobby. Or maybe you'd like to volunteer on a community storm-spotting team. But suppose you want to chase storms as part of your job. In that case, your best chance is to become a meteorologist. Then you could get a job at a national weather research center or a TV station. You might work for a company that designs weather instruments. They need to be tested in real storm conditions. Or you might

20

join a company that makes films or videos of storms. There are many ways you can contribute to the science of storm chasing.

You can prepare for a storm-chasing career by taking math and science classes. To work in a weather center, you will need a college degree in meteorology or a related field. Dozens of colleges and universities offer meteorology degrees. Others offer a degree in atmospheric sciences. This degree combines meteorology with other branches of science. University students are often involved in a weather center's storm intercept activities. This is a great way to get experience and on-the-job training.

Some storm chasers spend their lives in the "private club" of storm chasing. Not Warren Faidley. This journalist and photographer became the first full-time, professional storm chaser. At the same time, he connected his storm-chasing passion with larger issues. Over the years, he observed changes in global weather patterns. This led him to become a popular public speaker on global warming. Faidley also founded the Storm Angel Foundation. It educates children about storm safety and assists children who are victims of severe weather.

Many scientists in the meteorology field have degrees in **physics**, math, and other sciences. As a mathematician or computer scientist, you could design computer systems that show weather conditions. As a physicist, you might do research on lightning or winds. As an electrical engineer, you may design radars or other tornado-related instruments. All of these different roles can help expand tornado research.

Being a meteorologist can be exciting, even if you don't chase storms. You could provide valuable weather information to city governments, farmers, or sports teams. Working in a weather center, you would study weather patterns or forecast the weather. You might exchange weather information with other countries. You might even do research on air pollution or global warming. These are great ways to benefit people around the country and around the world.

CHAPTER FOUR

THE FUTURE OF STORM CHASING

A storm-spotting team videotapes an approaching storm. The film and other information will help the team learn more.

As long as there are tornadoes, we will always need storm chasers. People once had little or no warning that a tornado was coming. There wasn't much they could do to protect themselves. Now meteorologists can send out

Tornadoes and other violent storms can be deadly. Scientists are working to learn more about them so they can warn people earlier and save lives.

tornado warnings. Much of their information comes from storm-chasing scientists. That information saves lives.

Before the 1990s, the National Weather Service could issue tornado warnings only 5 or 6 minutes before a tornado struck. By 2005, the average warning time was almost 15 minutes. But meteorologists want to warn people much earlier than that. With better, faster weather information collected by meteorologists and storm chasers, more lives can be saved.

New types of radar could be the key to earlier warnings. The NSSL is testing radar systems that can scan weather conditions faster than ever before. Ideally, these radars would be mounted on vehicles. Then meteorologists could take them out to where a tornado seems to be forming.

Turtles are another concept for future development. Turtles are instruments that measure weather conditions inside a tornado. They are shaped like an upside-down bowl—or a turtle. Storm-chasing scientists try to place a turtle in the path of a tornado, hoping the storm passes over it. It's hard to know where a tornado will travel, though. Scientists hope to get better at knowing exactly where to place turtles.

Unmanned aerial vehicles (UAVs) have a great future in storm chasing, too. They're like airplanes or helicopters, only they have no pilot. An operator on the ground directs

Specially equipped trucks help storm chasers gather data in the field.

the UAV into the center of a storm. It gathers air and wind information that no other instrument can collect.

On the ground, chase vehicles of the future will carry or launch a fantastic collection of instruments. Weather information from all sources will come into the vehicle. From there, real-time information will go out to local or regional forecast offices.

These are just a few of the directions meteorologists hope to take in the future. All these developments make for better forecasting and earlier warnings. They also help meteorologists educate people about storm safety. Better tornado information is valuable to builders, too. It can guide them in designing homes, stores, and other buildings that can survive tornadoes.

Professional storm chasers do have one concern about the future of storm chasing. Since the movie *Twister* came out, hundreds of amateur chasers have invaded Tornado Alley. Many of them are safe and sensible. But others cause traffic jams, drive dangerously, run into

NSSL's VORTEX project—short for Verification of the Origin of Rotation in Tornadoes Experiment—took place in 1994 and 1995. It gathered massive amounts of information about why thunderstorms produce tornadoes. Team members were often outside their vehicle launching weather balloons. Their biggest hazard was lightning. Project leader Erik Rasmussen valued his team's safety more than anything else. If lightning was striking nearby, he would cancel a launch, even if it meant losing time and missing a valuable opportunity.

animals, knock down fences, and race across private land. They get in the way of professionals who have important jobs to do. Eager to get ever closer to tornadoes, they put themselves and others into danger.

These activities go against the spirit of storm chasing. Tornado Alley is no theme park. Storms should inspire a sense of wonder at the awesome forces of nature. Of course, chasing can be exciting, even for the most serious professionals. But their first goal is always to gather information—and to use that information to serve and protect their fellow humans.

SOME FAMOUS STORM CHASERS

Warren Faidley (1957–) is a photojournalist and the first professional storm chaser. Known for his adventurous chases, he provides photos and videos of severe storms through his company, Weatherstock Inc. Faidley's interests include global warming and disaster education.

David Hoadley (1938?–) is often called the father of storm chasing. His photos, articles, and storm information have been a great benefit to meteorologists. Hoadley founded *Storm Track*, the first storm chasers' magazine.

Roger Jensen (1933–2001) was a pioneer storm chaser. He began photographing storms when he was a teenager. As an adult, he was known for his photographs of tornadoes, thunderstorms, clouds, and other weather-related subjects.

Erik Rasmussen (?–) is one of the leading research scientists studying supercells and tornadoes at NSSL and the University of Oklahoma. He led the Verification of the Origin of Rotation in Tornadoes Experiment (VORTEX) project. It revealed massive amounts of information about why thunderstorms produce tornadoes.

Tim Samaras (1957–) is an engineer who designed the first turtle tornado-measuring instrument. In 2003, he successfully placed it directly in a tornado's path. Samaras continues to design equipment for NSSL and chase storms.

Neil Ward (1914–1972) was the first storm-chasing scientist. He began chasing storms as a hobby and later became a meteorologist with the NSSL. Ward built the first tornado simulator, which imitated the wind motion of tornadoes.

Joshua (Josh) Wurman (1960–) is one of the nation's top tornado, hurricane, and radar scientists. He developed the Doppler on Wheels (DOW) mobile radar. Wurman was president of the Center for Severe Weather Research (CSWR) in Boulder, Colorado, from 1998 to 2005.

GLOSSARY

amateur (AM-uh-chur) someone who takes part in an activity for enjoyment instead of for pay

atmospheric pressure (at-muh-SFIHR-ik PREH-shur) the force exerted by the weight of the air at a given location. Tornadoes develop in low-pressure conditions.

forecasts (FOR-kasts) reports about future weather conditions

funnel (FUHN-uhl) a cone-shaped tool, wide at the top and narrow at the bottom, for pouring liquids into a container

hobby (HOB-ee) an activity done in one's spare time for relaxation and enjoyment

intercept (in-tur-SEPT) to interrupt or stop something on its way from one place to another

labs (LABZ) places with the equipment and conditions for doing scientific studies; short for *laboratories*

physics (FIH-ziks) a science of matter, motion, and energy

professional (pruh-FESH-uh-nuhl) someone involved in an activity as a paid job

radar (RAY-dar) an instrument that sends and receives radio waves to detect distant objects

research (REE-surch) detailed scientific study to find out information about something

satellite (SA-tuh-lite) an object that circles Earth to send back signals or scientific information

volunteer (vol-uhn-TIHR) someone who chooses to do a helpful task for no pay

FOR MORE INFORMATION

Books

Davies, Jon. *Storm Chasers! On the Trail of Twisters.* Helena, MT: Farcountry Press, 2007.

Hammonds, Heather. *Meteorologists.* Mankato, MN: Smart Apple Media, 2004.

Jeffrey, Gary, and Gianluca Garofalo (illustrator). *Hurricane Hunters and Tornado Chasers.* NY: Rosen Central, 2008.

Woods, Michael, and Mary B. Woods. *Tornadoes.* Minneapolis, MN: Lerner Publications, 2007.

Web Sites

Extreme Weather Adventurer and Storm Chaser Warren Faidley
www.warrenfaidley.com/
Read more about expert storm chaser Warren Faidley

Sky Diary Kidstorm
www.skydiary.com/kids/
Learn more about tornadoes, hurricanes, lightning, and storm chasing

Tornadoes: Science with NOAA Research
www.oar.noaa.gov/k12/html/tornadoes2.html
For more information about tornadoes and tornado safety

INDEX

ABOUT THE AUTHOR

Ann Heinrichs is the author of more than 200 books for children and young adults. They cover U.S. and world history and culture, science and nature, and English grammar. Ann has also enjoyed careers as a children's book editor and an advertising copywriter. An avid traveler, she has toured Europe, Africa, the Middle East, and East Asia. Born in Fort Smith, Arkansas, she now lives in Chicago. She enjoys biking, kayaking, and flying kites.